Tropical cloud forests are one of the most interesting ecosystems in the world. They have an incredible variety of flora and fauna.

The cloud forests with their exuberant vegetation offer us a variety of beautiful plants of the families ARACEAE, HELICONIACEAE, CANNACEAE, GESNERIACEAE, BROMELIACEAE, ZINGIBERACEAE, ORCHIDACEAE..., and many ferns and bamboos.

Venezuela has many cloud forests in its numerous mountains, in particular in the Cordillera de los Andes and the Cordillera de la Costa. I have observed cloud forests in the states of Mérida, Lara, Aragua and Miranda.

Page 9. *Clusia* (CLUSIACEAE).

Page 10. The epiphyte *Guzmania* (BROMELIACEAE).

Pages 11 to 15. The bamboo *Arthrostylidium* (POACEAE).

Pages 16 and 17. Two different species of *Anthurium* (ARACEAE).

Pages 18 to 22. Ferns.

Page 23. *Chamaedorea pinnatifrons* (ARECACEAE).

Pages 24 to 27. *Renealmia thyrsoidea* (ZINGIBERACEAE):

Page 26. Inflorescences (yellow flowers and red bracteas) and fruits.

Page 27. Seedlings.

Page 28. Creek in a cloud forest.

Page 29. *Canna ottonis* (CANNACEAE). growing in a cloud forest creek bed.

Page 30. *Cyclanthus bipartitus* (CYCLANTHACEAE).

Page 31. *Govenia superba* (ORCHIDACEAE).

Page 32. *Sanicula liberta* (APIACEAE).

Pages 33 and 34. *Napeanthus apodemus* (GESNERIACEAE).

31

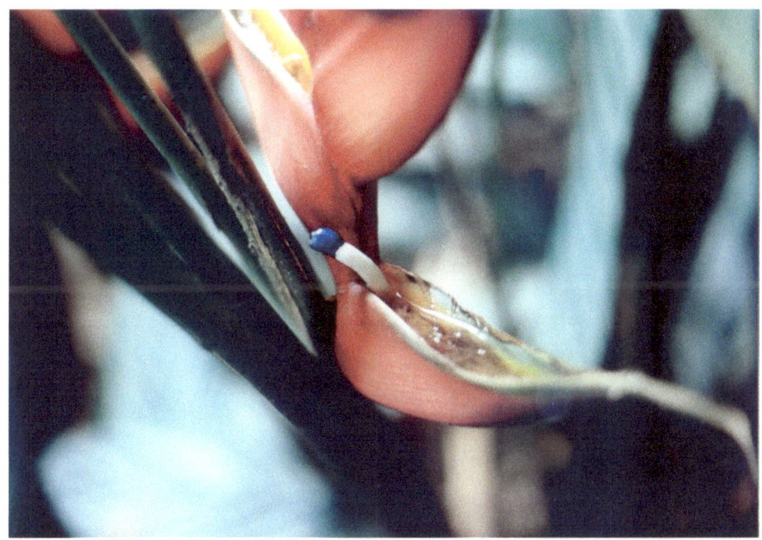